CATECHISM OF
ANIMAL MANAGEMENT, ETC.

LONDON:
PRINTED UNDER THE AUTHORITY OF HIS MAJESTY'S STATIONERY OFFICE.
By HARRISON AND SONS, 45-47, St. Martin's Lane, W.C.
PRINTERS IN ORDINARY TO HIS MAJESTY

FIRESTEP
Editions
www.firesteppublishing.com

FireStep Publishing
Gemini House
136-140 Old Shoreham Road
Brighton
BN3 7BD

www.firesteppublishing.com

First published by the General Staff, War Office 1916.
First published in this format by FireStep Editions,
an imprint of FireStep Publishing, in association with
the National Army Museum, 2013.

www.nam.ac.uk

ISBN 978-1-908487-69-8

Cover design FireStep Publishing
Typeset by FireStep Publishing
Printed and bound in Great Britain

Please note: *In producing in facsimile from original historical documents,
any imperfections may be reproduced and the quality may
be lower than modern typesetting
or cartographic standards.*

OFFICIAL COPY.

[Crown Copyright Reserved.

CATECHISM OF
ANIMAL MANAGEMENT, ETC.

LONDON:
PRINTED UNDER THE AUTHORITY OF HIS MAJESTY'S STATIONERY OFFICE
BY HARRISON AND SONS, 45-47, ST. MARTIN'S LANE, W.C.,
PRINTERS IN ORDINARY TO HIS MAJESTY.

To be purchased, either directly or through any Bookseller, from
WYMAN AND SONS, LIMITED, 29, BREAMS BUILDINGS, FETTER LANE, E.C., and
54, ST. MARY STREET, CARDIFF; or
H.M. STATIONERY OFFICE (SCOTTISH BRANCH), 23, FORTH STREET, EDINBURGH; or
E. PONSONBY, LIMITED, 116, GRAFTON STREET, DUBLIN;
or from the Agencies in the British Colonies and Dependencies,
the United States of America and other Foreign Countries of
T. FISHER UNWIN, LIMITED, LONDON, W.C.

1916.
Price One Penny.

CATECHISM OF ANIMAL MANAGEMENT, ETC.

Grooming.

To what points should a driver chiefly direct attention to ensure the welfare of his horses?—To their grooming, their feeding, their watering, and their care, whilst at exercise and drill.

Why is grooming important?—The natural perspiration and excretions through the skin of a horse are increased by high feeding and hard work; good grooming prevents the pores of the skin from becoming clogged by dust and dirt, thus allowing them to act freely.

What are the various articles used for grooming horses?—Body brushes, dandy brushes, curry combs, rubbers, sponges, and wisps.

Which is the best?—A body brush is the best, but the result is better if a wisp is used in addition.

How are wisps made?—By twisting hay, or straw, into a rope about three yards long, then forming two loops at one end, and twisting the free end round, and between each loop, until they are firmly united together.

When is a dandy brush preferable to a body brush?—In Camp, and for grooming heavy draught horses.

How should the brush be used?—Mostly with the natural direction of the hair.

What are curry-combs used for ?—They are used for cleaning the body brush.

What is the good of wisping ?—After the skin is thoroughly cleansed with a brush, a damp wisp, well laid on, gives the coat a good polish. If the coat is greasy, the wisp is sometimes better than a brush.

What is the best way of testing if a horse has been well groomed ?—By passing the fingers the reverse way through the direction of the hair, particularly behind the elbow and under the belly. If the horse is dirty, they will be covered with grey scurf.

Why should a horse be groomed at once after exercise ?—Exercise opens the pores ; the horse is then more liable to chill if left undried ; also, before the perspiration is caked on the skin, it is easier to remove.

What parts should be dried first ?—The heels first, then the legs, because they are more susceptible of chill than the body.

Should any parts of the horse be washed ?—Beyond sponging out such places, in which the brush cannot be used, such as the eyes, nostrils, and dock, it is only necessary to wash the feet. White and grey-legged horses, in dirty weather, require to have their legs washed sometimes, to clean the hair.

What precaution must invariably be taken after washing any part of the legs ?—To dry it at once, otherwise cracked heels, or grease, are frequently the result.

What is the effect of washing horses legs ?—If the weather is cold, or if there is a cold wind, cracked heels, greasy heels, or mud fever result if not at once dried.

What care should be taken of the back or loins, if the horse is hot when the legs are being cleaned?—If the saddle and pad have been ordered to be taken off, a sack or numnah should be put over the horse's back.

Where should this be placed?—It is better placed over the loins ; that is, rather in the rear of the position of the saddle, as it there protects these vital parts most frequently attacked by chill.

To what does neglect of grooming lead?—To skin disease and vermin.

Clipping.

When and why do horses cast their coats?—In the spring and in the autumn. The thick winter coat provides an extra warm covering for the winter months, which helps to maintain weight and condition. The summer coat being very fine, prevents excessive sweating in the hot weather.

Why are horses clipped in the winter?—Under natural conditions horses do not sweat in the winter, but when they are required to work hard, a thick heavy coat keeps them in constant sweat and prevents them being dried quickly after work.

Why should they be dried quickly after work?—To prevent chill.

Are there any other evils arising from horses having long coats, when in stables?—They require more labour in grooming, and the coat is liable to harbour skin disease.

Why are some horses only clipped trace high?—This is suitable for horses that work only at a walk and therefore do not sweat very much.

Why are the legs left unclipped?—Because the legs of horses do not sweat and the long hair keeps the legs warm.

Has clipping any effect on the amount of food given?—Yes. It is equal to two pounds of oats per day which it would be necessary to give to maintain the horse in condition if he had a long heavy coat.

How many times is it necessary to clip horses in the winter?—Twice a year, in November and January or February, depending upon the growth of the coat.

Watering.

How many times a day should horses be watered?—Three times a day at least, before each feed.

How much does a horse drink at a time?—About three or four gallons, but at early morning stables only half this quantity is usually taken.

How long does it take a horse to drink?—About five minutes.

If water is given after feeding, what may often be the result?—An attack of colic or gripes.

May horses be watered when they are hot?—Yes, in moderation, if they are out and are not to be worked at a fast pace immediately.

What then should be done on arrival in stables after a march or field day?—As the men are generally sent to their rooms to change, the horses must be left standing for some time. They should, therefore, be watered sparingly, say about half a bucketful; if very hot and sweating much, they should be given none at all.

Why may horses be watered fully in one case but only sparingly in another?—Because a long draught of cold water gives a sudden chill to the system overheated by exertion. If the horse is kept warm by exercise or grooming the chill is overcome.

What is the result of trotting to water from and to stables?— It may cause colic or loss of condition.

What should be done about watering horses on a march?— They may be watered frequently, especially if the weather is hot, but they must not be worked at a fast pace afterwards.

Should they be allowed to drink freely?—Yes, if allowed to drink freely from the outset, there is little fear of them drinking more than they ought when fatigued.

What care must be taken about the water?—Be careful about public troughs to which every animal on the road has access. Glanders, farcy, and other infectious diseases may often be contracted by neglecting this.

Feeding.

How many times a day should horses be fed?—At least three times, or four if possible.

Why is it preferable to feed four times daily?—Because horses have small stomachs compared with other animals. It is, therefore, natural for them to eat in small quantities and often.

What would be the result of giving a double feed to a horse that has missed a feed?—It might result in colic or some other illness of the bowels.

What should be given with each feed of corn at all times?—A couple of handfuls of chopped straw and hay.

Why?—Horses, especially greedy feeders, are apt to bolt their corn, which makes it difficult of proper digestion. When the corn is mixed with chaff, this is prevented, as it is difficult for a horse to bolt chaff, and it ensures thorough mastication of the food.

Is it sufficient for the feed thus prepared to be just thrown into the manger?—No ; it should be stirred with the hand to mix the chaff and oats together.

If no chaff is available is there any other way of preventing horses bolting their food?—A small quantity of hay given before the oats will take the keenness off their appetite and make them eat more slowly.

What else should a driver ascertain?—That his horses get their proper share of corn ; some are rapid feeders, and, having finished their own share, eat half of their neighbours. Others put their heads first into their neighbour's mangers, while some toss their corn about and throw it out of the manger.

What is the best way of making sure that each horse gets his proper share?—By seeing that all horses are secured on the short rack before giving the feed.

What is the usual quantity of food for a horse to receive at each meal?—Five to six pounds, of which three pounds would be oats and the remainder hay.

Why do horses receive less food in the morning than in the evening?—Because it is injurious for them to do fast or severe work when gorged with food, and they have more time to eat and digest food during the night.

When should a bran mash be given?—It is usual to give a bran mash on Saturday evening stable hour in place of corn, as it is less heating and opens the horse's bowels slightly.

How is a bran mash made?—By scalding 2 to 3 lbs. of bran in a bucket, with boiling water, then covering it with a piece of sack, or rug, and allowing it to stand until cool enough to eat.

For what purpose is linseed given to horses?—To fatten, and to improve the coat in those that are "hide-bound."

In what forms can linseed be given?—Soaked, or boiled, and as linseed cake, or linseed oil.

Is there any difference between soaked and boiled linseed?—No. It is impossible to tell the difference between linseed which has been soaked in cold water for 24 hours and linseed which has been slowly boiled for 12 hours; the feeding effects are the same.

How should linseed cake be given?—Crushed.

What is the effect of feeding with green grass?—In small quantities it is beneficial, and when a horse is sick, or doing no work, it is excellent food, but if horses are worked hard after eating too much, it purges them, and causes loss of condition.

Is straw ever given as a food to horses?—Yes. It is a common and good practice to save 2 lbs. of oat straw, and make it into chaff to mix with the food.

Is barley ever given to horses?—Yes. In the East it is the ordinary food, but imported horses have to become gradually accustomed to it.

When, and in what quantities is it customary to give it in England?—Every evening, from 2 to 4 lbs..of boiled barley are frequently given in England, to very thin horses.

How are the horses fed?—Usually three times a day, viz., morning, midday, and evening.

Morning, 2 lbs. of hay and 3 lbs. of oats.
Midday, 3 lbs. „ „ 3 lbs. „
Evening, 5 lbs. „ „ 4 lbs. „

With extra ration 1 lb. of oats is added to the morning feed, and 1 lb. to the evening feed. In addition 2 lbs. of hay is chopped up and given with the oats at each feed. Sometimes four feeds a day are better.

What is the best way of dealing with thin horses?—Feed little and often; vary the food with bran, linseed, maize, and barley; try crushed oats; let them have water constantly by them, and ease off their work. Teeth should be examined and filed if sharp.

How does exercise benefit such horses?—It helps to regulate the bowels, and make the muscles firm and hard.

Why is it dangerous to take a horse to work if it is noticed he has not finished his morning feed?—Because he may be in the first stage of fever, or some disease, and to work him in this state would probably result in a long and serious illness.

To what other points should a man give his attention?—To keeping the mangers clean; dirt, gravel, oil rags, fragments of the litter, stale corn, or the sour remains of a bran mash, make a horse's food unwholesome, and put him off his feed.

When should the nosebag be taken off?—As soon as the horse has done feeding. Unless this is attended to he cannot breathe freely, and by lowering his head to the ground, and rubbing about with his muzzle to pick up any stray oats in the bottom of the bag, he wears the bag out.

Care of Horses on the March and in Billets.

How do you know when a horse is not in condition?—He is either very thin, or fat and flabby, and tires very soon.

What is a horse like when he is tired?—Some roll about in their walk or trot; some drag their legs and stumble, others sweat too much, or get distressed in their breathing.

What is the effect of working horses when tired?—They may fall and break their knees, or if called upon for an extra effort, may sprain their tendons.

Is it necessary for horses to be idle when in poor condition?—No; they are better for walking exercise twice daily.

What injury to horses is most to be feared and needs the greatest care to prevent on the line of march?—Galls.

What are the most common causes of galls?—Soft condition, new or badly fitting saddles or harness; also lolling in the saddle.

In what place is a gall most difficult to cure?—On the back or withers.

What are the best means of preventing it?—Pay great attention to the stuffing and position of the saddle, to the sit of the numnah, and to riding.

What are the chief places in which galls occur?—On the withers and back; on the shoulders from the collar; under the belly from the girth; trace galls; curb chain galls; and under the tail from the crupper. In wheel horses the breeching sometimes causes a chafe, but this may always be seen while marching. The mess tin sometimes chafes, as also does the crupper. Most of these can be entirely avoided if the harness and the appointments be properly fitted and put on before starting.

What causes girth gall?—The girths buckled too far forward, or the surcingle too tight under it, causing it to wrinkle.

What is to be done to galls?—Remove the cause as far as possible and apply salt and water frequently, provided the skin is not broken.

If a gall begins to appear, how may it be checked?—Sometimes by altering the fit of the harness. Sometimes by using leather pads or pieces of sheepskin to keep pressure from the spot. A supply of these should be provided by the collar makers previous to the march.

How may galls be prevented?—Assuming that the harness and appointments have been properly fitted before starting, care should be taken during the march, to see that there is no shifting of the pad, and that the rider maintains a steady seat in his saddle. Lolling too and fro in the saddle is a frequent source of sore back. When the " Halt " is sounded, care should be taken to carry out the order " Lookround." A slight rub under the collar, on the back, or withers, or under the girth, may be checked at once by being attended to on the spot. Much future trouble in fomenting and dressing may thus be spared to the driver himself.

What steps are taken to detect galls or lameness after a march?—As soon as the saddles and pads are off, every part of the horses' backs and bellies should be carefully felt, and the slightest chafe or lump should be reported as soon as possible, and all orders relative to them must be carefully carried out to prepare the horses for the following day's march. Any swelling in the legs, or lameness, should be detected before the arrival of the officer, and should be reported.

What points must be seen to inside stables where billeted?— See that the ventilation is good, and that there is a bale up between each horse. If bales are not available you must tie your horses up, so that they cannot hurt one another, or be hurt by their neighbours, or by any horses standing on the opposite side of the stable. It must be remembered that all horses are apt to be nervous on coming into a new stable, and they will sometimes kick horses that they are in the habit of standing next to.

What next should the driver attend to?—After having tied up his horses he should do the same as is customary in his barracks, go on with his work, and not leave his billet until visited, and permission has been obtained. As it often happens in inferior stabling that there are loose bricks or stones covering the drains, the driver should look round and satisfy himself on these points, so that there may be no danger of his horses putting their feet on them. He should also assure himself that the rack and manger fittings are tolerably secure, and that there is a means of locking the doors of the stables and harness room.

Should the driver feel dissatisfied with the accommodation or be unable to comply with any orders he has received, what should he do?—It is better for him to avoid, as far as possible, all personal reference to the landlord or owner of the stable, and he should wait until the arrival of his section sergeant, who ought soon to visit him, and to whom he should report any deficiencies.

What about the driver's own dinner ?—He should waste no unnecessary time over it, but should begin grooming his horses as soon as possible after they have finished their feeds. If their legs are very wet, he should dry the heels and legs before going to his dinner. The horse should be his first care.

At what pace does a horse walk or trot ?—The average pace of the walk is four miles an hour, and the trot six miles an hour.

Is it injurious for a horse to trot faster than six miles an hour ?—Not if it is limited to a short distance, but if continued for long, the horse may hurt himself, or stumble or fall.

What is the effect of fast work on the condition of horses ?— In moderation it has no harmful effect, but if continuous they lose condition.

After the horses are groomed, what should be done to them ?— They may be fully watered when quite cool, and again before feeding ; bedded down, fed at the proper time, and be left as quiet as possible ; the driver should be satisfied as to their security throughout the night.

If a horse should begin to shake or tremble after having been watered, what had better be done ?—Let him be groomed vigorously under the belly and on the flanks with a good wisp of dry straw. But should the horse show no signs of getting better after a few minutes, he should be led about and kept moving, and the farrier called with as little delay as possible. In all cases the matter must be reported to him, or the section sergeant, or shoeing smith, when he next comes round.

What must the driver be careful to ascertain about the next day's march ?—The hour when he is expected to "hook in" at the wagon park ; he is always to carry a feed of corn with him for his horses at the midday halt.

In the morning, how are the horses best prepared for the day's march ?—The driver should take care to be up early enough to let them have their morning feeds comfortably, then to put the harness and appointments on, and to turn out of the stables in time to walk quietly down to the wagon park, properly dressed and equipped.

NOTE.—It happens from time to time that drivers have to march with horses either entirely alone, as with a horse which has been left behind sick, or under the command of a non-commissioned officer, as with remounts. The following questions are asked with a view to their instruction under such circumstances.

At what hour should the start be made in the morning ?— Generally, so that the day's march be finished about 1 p.m. In very hot weather, or if the march be a long one of twenty-five miles or upwards, the start must be made earlier, always remembering that the horse must be well fed and cared for on the journey.

When should feeds be carried on the march ?—Whenever absence from Camp or quarters is likely to exceed four hours.

How long a halt should be made to feed ?—Not more than three-quarters of an hour, this gives time to water, and feed, and for the driver himself to get something to eat.

When should halts be made ?—It is well to make the first halt after having gone a mile. A good look-round should then be made and, if all is correct, future stoppages should be for about ten minutes every hour.

Feet.

What is to be done if a horse suddenly goes lame?—Get off and examine the foot to see if there is a stone in it, or if a nail has been picked up. If no apparent cause can be seen, apply a cold water bandage above, and on the fetlock, on arrival in stables, as the injury is most likely a sprain.

Why should the feet be picked out daily?—To prevent thrush, which is a foul discharge from the cleft of the frog, and to remove stones, or any nails which may have been picked up at work.

How are the feet affected by standing on dirty bedding?—In addition to causing thrush, the feet become very soft, and easily break, making it difficult to shoe the horse.

What are corns?—Bruises in the heels of the feet, generally caused by leaving the shoes on too long.

What is the remedy for greasy heels?—Clean them well with tepid water, and put on a bran or oatmeal poultice, keeping it on all night.

If a horse is pricked in the foot, what must be done?—Get a shoeing smith, if possible, and personally see the shoe removed; then apply a bran poultice.

What is the weight of a horse shoe?—From $1\frac{3}{4}$ to $2\frac{1}{4}$ lbs.

How often is a horse shod?—Once a month, or oftener if required.

How often should a horse's shoes be examined?—Every morning and on coming in from a march or duty.

First Aid.

Why do horses rub and bite themselves?—As a rule this is due to bad grooming, but it may also be due to mange or some skin disease.

What should you do if you notice your horse rubbing or biting himself?—Report it to the Section Sergeant immediately so that the horse can be sent to the Sick Lines for inspection.

Why is this necessary?—Because mange is contagious, and unless the horse is isolated immediately the disease would quickly spread to all the other horses.

What other form of contagious skin disease is prevalent amongst army horses?—Ringworm.

What is the first sign of ringworm?—Small raised circular patches of hair, which soon come off, leaving bare places.

What is the best way of preventing mange and ringworm?—Regular clipping and grooming, when it is easier to recognise and control cases.

How do horses catch colds?—By being in a hot and stuffy stable and afterwards standing about in the open.

How would you know if a horse has a cold?—He would cough and perhaps have a discharge from his nostrils and eyes.

What is the cure for a cold?—Well steam the nostrils with hay soaked in a bucket of hot water, after which the head should be thoroughly dried, and a stimulant should be applied to the throat. This may be rubbed in again in the morning, but the nostrils must not be steamed before going out. Particular attention must be paid to keeping the nostrils clean. Care must be taken that the sponge used for this horse is not used for any other, and they must be watered separately.

How is "steaming nostrils" done?—Place some hay or bran in a bucket and pour in boiling water ; hold the horse's nose over the pail, and put a cloth over his head to keep in the steam. When finished be careful to dry the horse's head well. This must not be done within two hours of the horse leaving the stable, and therefore should not be done in the morning before marching. If bran is used, hay should always be put over it to prevent the horse scalding his lips and tongue.

Why should horses with discharge from the nostrils, not be allowed to drink from the same trough or bucket as other horses?—Because they may infect other horses with their colds.

What is the proper course for a man to take should he notice the slightest injury to his horse, or anything at all unusual with him?—He should at once inform his Section Sergeant.

What is the use of rubbing a horse's legs by hand?—It excites the circulation of the blood where the circulation is most feeble.

When should this be resorted to?—When the horse is unable to be exercised by reason of wet, frost, &c., and when the legs are "filled" at all from overwork.

Suppose a horse gets kicked, what treatment should be given?— Well cleanse the place, and foment with hot water if there is much hair.

If a horse breaks its knee, what is to be done?—Well cleanse the wound with tepid water, and be careful to see that all the grit is out. Hang a linen cloth, kept well wetted with cold water, loosely over the injured knee.

What is to be done with bandages for a horse's legs?—All cold water bandages should be made of linen, not of flannel, and must not be allowed to remain on all night, in case the leg swells and the bandage becomes too tight, and bandages cannot well be kept wet throughout the night.

If a horse's eye appears to be injured, what must be done?—Examine the eye carefully for a hay seed or other cause. If anything is found, remove it with a clean sponge, sponge the eye and hang a wet linen cloth over it to keep it cool; frequently soak the cloth in cold water.

How may colic symptoms be known?—If the horse rolls about in the stable, or shakes or breaks out in perspiration on the belly, or flanks, or otherwise shows signs of pain without apparent cause.

What is the treatment for colic?—A "colic draught," if provided, and, in any case, a hot bran mash must be given and the belly well rubbed with a wisp by two men, one on each side. The horse should be well groomed all over, then littered down, and a rug of some sort thrown over his back. Should he not get better within an hour, a veterinary surgeon must be called.

How is a "colic draught" to be given?—Two men are necessary for this; one must hold the horse's head well up in the air, while the other man, having the draught all ready (in a soda-water bottle or, preferably, a proper drenching horn) shakes it up and places the neck of the bottle in the horse's mouth at the rear of the teeth, and allows a portion of the medicine to flow into the throat. As soon as any drops begin to trickle from the mouth, the bottle must be withdrawn and the mouth kept closed until the medicine is swallowed. This operation must be repeated until the draught is all gone, and care must be taken, otherwise much of it is wasted. Should the horse be restive, more assistance must be obtained, and a "twitch" placed under his upper lip. Most civilian horsekeepers have one.

How is a common poultice prepared?—Take a handful of bran and add sufficient boiling water to soften it. Place the mixture in a strong cloth, apply at once to the part required and tie on. If a poultice is required for the foot, the foot should be soaked in hot water for half an hour before the poultice is applied.

How is a "stimulant" to be applied to the throat?—Some of the liniment must be poured into the palm of the hand and well rubbed in, round the under side of the joining of the head and neck, underneath the jowl, and for about six inches down the neck itself on the underpart. Rubbing should last from ten minutes to a quarter of an hour at a time.

What should be done if a fire threatens the safety of the horses?—Each horse should immediately be blindfolded with a horse rubber or other convenient cloth and led to a place of safety, there to await orders.

Why should the horses be blindfolded?—Horses are particularly nervous about fire, and it has been found that unless this precaution is adopted, they are liable to rush back to their stalls.

What points regarding the stable fittings should receive attention?—Each driver should see that the rack chains, collar chains, logs and bales are secure, and properly fitted, and he should be specially careful that no hooks or nails project from wooden bales or heel posts, which could possibly injure the horse. Many horses' eyes have been lost through neglecting this.

NOTES ON HARNESS.

1. *Saddle.*—Should be placed on the middle of the horse's back, so that the front arch is above the hollow behind the shoulder; the front edge of the side bars being about the breadth of a hand behind the play of the shoulder (the luggage saddle about two hands' breadth).

The front of the saddle should not be so far forward that it interferes with the play of the shoulder. The pannels of the saddle should lie flat on the top of the horse's ribs, the weight of the rider being borne by the part between the front and back arches. The burrs and fans should bear no weight. The front arch, when numnah or stuffed panels are attached, should clear the withers to the breadth of not less than two fingers when the rider is in saddle. The saddle, to afford a suitable seat for the rider, should be level, neither dipped in front nor in rear.

2. *Girth.*—Should only be tight enough to keep the saddle in its place. It should be tightened gradually and not with violence, care being taken that the skin is not wrinkled. When buckled, it should just allow of a finger being placed between the girth and the edge of breast bone.

3. *Surcingle.*—Should lie flat over and be not tighter than the girth.

4. *Saddle Blanket.*—Can be folded in several ways. With a horse of normal shape and condition the following method is recommended :—Fold lengthways in three folds; one end is then turned over twenty-four inches, and the other turned into pocket formed by the folds. The blanket is then placed on the horse's back, with the thick part near the withers, but raised well off them by putting the hand under the blanket.

5. *Numnah.*—When used, must be raised well into the

space between the numnah pannels or stuffed pannels with the hand and arm, and when means are provided, fastened in this position.

6. *Stirrup.*— Attached to the saddle as follows :—The end of the stirrup leather is passed through the stirrup iron, then through the link on side bar of saddle from below, inwards to outwards, then fastened to tongue of buckle. The buckle is then pulled up close to the link on side bar, the point of stirrup leather passed between the two leathers from the front, then passed under the surcingle.

7. *Traces.*—Should be of equal length, otherwise collar galls will occur. Their length in wheel must, in a great measure, depend upon the size of horses, and particular vehicle to which they are attached.

8. *Head Collar.*—The cheek piece should be parallel to and behind the projecting cheek bone, the throat lash should fit loosely, being only sufficiently tight to prevent the head collar slipping over the horse's ears. (A good guide is the breadth of a hand between it and the horse's cheek.) The nose band should be two finger-breadths below the cheek bone and should admit two fingers between it and the nose.

9. *Bit.*—Should be adjusted into the horse's mouth in such a manner that the mouthpiece is above the tush or corner teeth, and that when the reins are pulled the curb chain lies in the chin groove and not above it. The smooth side of the mouthpiece should be next the horse's tongue.

These instructions can only be laid down as a general guide, as so much depends upon the shape and sensitiveness of the horse's mouth and on his temper.

In case of doubt it is better to adjust the bit too high than too low in the mouth. If too high it merely injures the skin at the angles of the lips, but too low a bit very frequently causes grave injury to the gums and even to the bone of the jaw.

On active service when a horse looses flesh the bit tends to hang lower in the mouth, and re-adjustment is necessary as a rule to prevent bit injury. Also new leather tends to stretch with wear, and this also causes the bit to hang lower as the cheek straps lengthen.

10. *Bridoon.*—Should touch the corners of the mouth but not wrinkle them.

11. *Curb.*—Should lie flat and smooth in the chin groove and be so adjusted that when the bit is pulled back to its greatest extent, the angle which the bit forms with the mouth should never exceed half a right angle, even with the lightest mouthed horse, and should vary between that and 30 degrees according to the degree of harshness of mouth. A guide often used is to ascertain that two fingers can be admitted between the curb and the horse's jawbone when the cheeks of the bit are in line, and the rein is quite loose.

The curb chain is fixed permanently on the off curb hook and the adjustment to the near curb hook is made by twisting the chain to the right until it is quite flat, putting the last link on the hook with the back of the thumb up, and then shortening the chain to the desired length, putting the selected link on with the back of the thumb down.

12. *Riding Rein for Draught Horses.*—Should be fitted at such a length that when held by the middle in the full of the left hand, the driver has complete control over his horse.

13. *Side Rein.*—Is buckled to the cheek of bit, passed through the keeper on the neck collar, and then buckled to the off side of luggage saddle. It should have a light feeling on the off side of the horse's mouth when the head is straight.

14. *Leading Rein.*—Is buckled to the bit, the short piece on the near side, and should be of sufficient length not to check the horse in its work.

The bearing of the bit in the horse's mouth must be even when the rein is held in the driver's hand.

15. *Neck Collar.*—Should be fitted so as to allow the flat of the hand to pass freely between it and the lower part of the horse's neck, and just room for the fingers to pass between it and the horse's neck at the sides.

16. *Breast Collar.*—When worn in place of the neck collar, to hang horizontally from the neck straps, the lower edge about one inch above the point of the shoulder, and should admit of the breadth of the hand between it and the horse's chest.

17. *Hames.*—Should be so bent as to fit neatly into the grooves of the neck collar, with both shoulders in line. The spare links should be so hooked that the hame strap, when buckled, will keep the shoulder hooks at the proper height. The points of the straps should lie inwards. Care must be taken that the pole chain ring is free.

18. *Wither Strap.*—Should not be tight, otherwise it will pull the saddle forward.

19. *Carrying Straps.*—Support the traces when out of draught ; must be loose when in draught.

20. *Hip Straps.*—The tugs are buckled in the desired slot in the breeching, and the hip straps are then fitted so as to keep the breeching in proper position.

21. *Breeching.*—Should lie horizontally from 14 to 16 inches below the upper part of the dock, and when the horses are hooked in should have a space, the breadth of the hand, between it and the horse's hind quarters.

22. *Back and Belly Band with tugs.*—To be of such a length that the points of shaft are carried the height of shoulder of hames, and to allow the breadth of a hand between it and the horse's belly when in draught.

Harnessing.

First Method.

(When the whole of the harness is not buckled together.)

Before commencing to harness, see (*a*) that the girths are buckled to the tabs on off side of the saddle, the surcingle is passed up through the keeper on off side of girth, that the surcingle and girth are tied in a loose knot to keep them clear of the ground, the crupper is attached, carrying straps are affixed, and wither strap looped on ; (*b*) that the luggage saddle is similarly equipped, also, with the back and belly band carrying the tugs ; (*c*) that the driving, leading, and side reins are attached to the bits, the driving and leading reins buckled so that the connecting buckles are between the horses ; (*d*) that the hames, complete with hame straps, and wither buckles, are fitted to the neck collars, but that the hame and housing straps are left unbuckled ; (*e*) that the traces are complete with leather pieces, rope and rear releasable attachment ; (*f*) that the curb is hanging loose.

The several parts as completed are placed on the horse in the following order :—blanket or numnah, saddle or luggage saddle, neck collar and hames, chain, hame attachment, breeching, traces (off side first), head collar, bit.

Numnah or blanket.—Place the numnah well up over the withers, and then draw it back to the required position, or fold the blanket and proceed in a similar manner. This causes the hair to lie in the natural position.

Saddle or luggage saddle.—Support it on the left arm, with the cantle towards the elbow and the crupper over the seat, held there by the right hand. Place it on the horse's back from the off side, the right hand assisting, and cast off the knot of girth and surcingle. Move round to the near side, if a dockpiece is used for the crupper, place it under the tail, gathering the tail hairs in the right hand before doing so, then move towards the animal's head, lift the saddle clear of the back towards the wither, work the numnah or blanket into the fork of saddle, and replace the saddle in the proper position with the sweat flaps lying flat and not doubled up, then buckle the girth and surcingle, and, in the case of the luggage saddle, also the back and belly band.

Neck collar and hames.—Place on the neck, housing of neck collar down, buckle housing strap and hame strap, keeping the wither buckle in position. Then bring the neck collar on to the smaller part of the neck, and turn with the mane, afterwards connecting the wither strap and wither buckle. Then hook on the "chain hame attachments."

Breeching.—Throw it across the loins from the off side, buckle up hip strap to tug, then move round to the near side and attach near hip strap to its tug.

Traces.—Commence with the off trace. Support the rope portion over the left forearm ; engage the front releasable attachment with the chain hame attachment, place the rope portion through the carrying straps, then buckle the breeching straps to the trace and breeching iron on the leather part of trace. When putting on the trace for the near side, the rope is carried over the right forearm. When not hooked into a vehicle the rope must be coupled up so as to keep clear of the ground by hooking it through the swivel eye at the end of the leather piece.

Head collar.—Turn the horse left about, and put on the head collar, buckling the throat lash. Then fasten head rope.

Bit.—Buckle to the off chape, then open the horse's mouth with the right hand, put the bit in the mouth, and buckle to near chape. Then adjust the curb chain as before described, and buckle the side rein.

Second Method.

(When the whole of the harness is buckled together.)

Before commencing see that the parts are put together as described in the preliminaries for the first method, except that the housing straps of neck collar and the hame straps are buckled, that the breeching is affixed to the crupper, and the bit to the offside of head collar.

On the command, "Harness up," turn the horse to the left about, take hold of the neck collar with both hands (one on each side), and put it on the neck, turning it in the manner before described, and hook on the chains, hame attachment, to the shoulder hooks of hames. Then place the numnah or blanket on the back, put on the saddle, or luggage saddle, raising the numnah or blanket well over the withers into the front arch, secure the girth and surcingle, and straighten out the crupper and breeching. Afterwards put on and secure the traces, buckling the breeching straps to the trace and breeching iron, put on the head collar, place the bit in the horse's mouth, adjust the curb chain, and fasten the head rope.

Unharnessing.—The horse is placed in the stall "heads about," and after the head collar and bit have been removed, is turned about, the stable head collar is put on, and the animal is placed on the short rack.

Unharnessing then takes place in the following order :—near trace, off trace, breeching, collar and hames, saddle, blanket or numnah.

Care of Harness.

Reasonable care should be exercised in the handling of articles of harness and saddlery. Saddles should not be dropped or thrown about, as fractured arches or broken side bars may result ; the throat of the neck collar is weakened, or even broken by unduly stretching the top part, a rifle bucket may damage the rifle itself if bent out of shape ; and the usefulness of a wither pad is quite destroyed when the article is subjected to unfair usage.

1. Bits, or any steel or ironwork subject to rust, should be wiped over on return to stables or camp, then well rubbed with an oil rag, as much after-time and trouble is saved if this is done before rust has time to form.

2. Ropes when dirty should be scrubbed, web girths require scrubbing with cold water to remove the sweat—saddle blankets or felt numnahs are to be placed in the sun or wind to dry, and then well beaten and brushed. Stuffed pannels must be put out to dry, then beaten, and rubbed with the hand to keep the stuffing in its place ; handles of drivers' whips may be scrubbed and the thongs and wrist guards sponged with water ; thongs of all whips require to be occasionally soft soaped to keep them supple.

3. *Leather Work.*—It is very rarely necessary to scrub leather work ; washing quickly in luke-warm water with soap, and, without soaking, is all that is necessary, even when harness or saddlery is very dirty, and, by adopting this process, the face of the leather is preserved.

Soda is very harmful to leather, and very hot water destroys its vitality. Whenever possible it is wise to limit the use of water, but parts affected by sweat from the horse, *i.e.*, inside surfaces of neck and breast collars, girths, certain straps, &c., should be sponged after use with clean cold water, allowed to dry, and then soaped on the inside. Leather should never be subjected to heat from fire, as its durable properties are destroyed.

There is no objection to a polish being given to the grain (outer side) of leather articles commonly used in the service, provided the flesh (under side) is kept mellow by the use of good yellow soap.

Soft soap contains an excess of alkali, and should be sparingly used, as otherwise leather is turned very dark and presents a sodden appearance. It should be worked into a lather and applied with a sponge.

Dubbin preserves leather, but its application is only necessary occasionally. It should be used every six months, harness or saddlery being taken to pieces, and, after the leather work has been cleaned, the dubbing should be applied. The leather work should be moistened with a sponge as absorption is promoted thereby, and in cold weather the dubbing should be applied warm. After laying by for two or three days, the residue of tallow on the surface should be brushed off. Saddle seats and flaps, rifle buckets, the outer covering of neck collars and parts which are to be kept stiff, require only lightly dubbing.

All leather work, before putting into store, should be dubbed.

As the safety of a gun or vehicle may depend on the strength of a strap, every endeavour should be made to keep harness in good condition and repair.

Minor defects in harness or saddlery should be attended to at once. Stitching should be tested from time to time, as the life of thread is shorter than leather. Girth tabs require special attention, and, with stirrup leathers, wear on fresh holes should be arranged for when requisite.

ND - #0531 - 270225 - C0 - 130/105/3 - PB - 9781908487698 - Matt Lamination